JUPITER

by Ruth Owen

WINDMILL BOOKS

New York

Published in 2014 by Windmill Books, An Imprint of Rosen Publishing
29 East 21st Street, New York, NY 10010

Produced for Windmill by Ruby Tuesday Books Ltd
Editor for Ruby Tuesday Books Ltd: Mark J. Sachner
US Editor: Joshua Shadowens
Designer: Alix Wood
Consultant: Kevin Yates, Fellow of the Royal Astronomical Society

Photo Credits:
Cover, 1, 4–5, 7 (bottom), 11, 12–13, 14–15, 16–17, 18–19, 21, 23, 24–25, 26–27, 28–29 © NASA; 6–7 © Shutterstock; 8–9 © Superstock.

Library of Congress Cataloging-in-Publication Data

Owen, Ruth, 1967–
Jupiter / by Ruth Owen.
     pages cm. — (Explore outer space)
Includes index.
ISBN 978-1-61533-726-2 (library binding) — ISBN 978-1-61533-769-9 (pbk.) —
ISBN 978-1-61533-770-5
1. Jupiter (Planet)—Juvenile literature. 2. Jupiter (Planet)—Exploration—Juvenile literature.
3. Galileo Project—Juvenile literature. I. Title. II. Series: Owen, Ruth, 1967– Explore outer space.
QB661.O935 2014
523.45—dc23

2013013475

Manufactured in the United States of America

CPSIA Compliance Information: Batch #BS13WM: For Further Information contact Windmill Books, New York, New York at 1-866-478-0556

CONTENTS

THE KING OF THE PLANETS

Jupiter is the fifth **planet** from the Sun and the most massive planet in the **solar system.**

It's impossible to comprehend the size of our own planet, but Jupiter's enormous size is truly mind-blowing. If you could drive a car at 60 miles per hour (97 km/h), day and night without stopping, it would take just over two weeks to drive around Earth's **equator.** To drive around giant Jupiter, however, would take six months! In fact, if Earth's diameter is compared to Jupiter's, the giant planet has a diameter that's 11 times the size of Earth's.

Jupiter is hundreds of millions of miles (km) from Earth. It is so large, though, that it is actually possible to see Jupiter without the need for a telescope. This means the earliest humans would have looked up into the night sky and been able to see the king of the planets shining brightly.

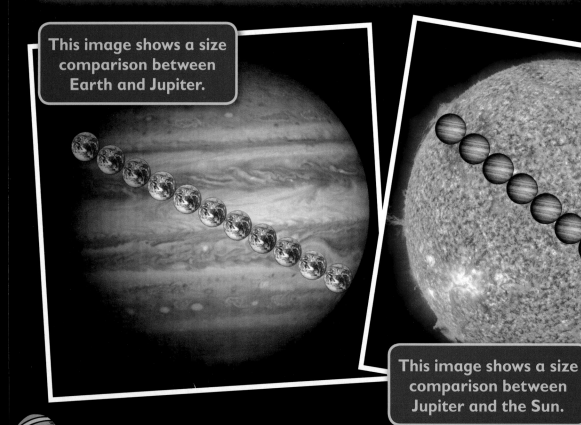

This image shows a size comparison between Earth and Jupiter.

This image shows a size comparison between Jupiter and the Sun.

This image of Jupiter was created using images captured by the spacecraft *Cassini* in December 2000.

That's Out of This World!

Jupiter may be the solar system's largest planet, but when compared to the Sun, it looks tiny. In fact, if the Sun were the size of a bowling ball, Jupiter would be smaller than a ping-pong ball.

THE BIRTH OF A PLANET

About five billion years ago, Jupiter, Earth, the other six planets in the solar system, and even the Sun did not exist.

The chemical ingredients to make the Sun and everything in our solar system did exist, however. These ingredients were floating in space in a vast cloud of gas and dust called a **nebula**.

Over millions of years, part of the cloud began to collapse on itself, forming a massive rotating sphere, or ball. A disk formed around the sphere from the remaining gas and dust. The material in the sphere was pressed together by **gravity**, causing it to heat up and pressure to build. Eventually, the heat and pressure became so great that the sphere ignited, and became a star. This new star was our Sun.

Gas and dust continued to spin in a disk around the newly formed star. Over time, material in the disk clumped together to form four rocky planets and four planets made mostly of gas, plus the **moons**, **asteroids**, and every other object in the solar system.

This diagram of our solar system shows the order of the eight planets from the Sun. The sizes of the planets are not to scale.

Mars

Venus

Earth

Mercury

That's Out of This World!

Mercury, Venus, Earth, and Mars are the planets that formed closest to the Sun. All four planets have solid, rocky surfaces. Jupiter, Saturn, Uranus, and Neptune, the furthest planets from the Sun, are made mostly of gas and do not have a solid surface. These huge planets are known as the gas giants.

Neptune

Uranus

Saturn

Jupiter

The sizes of the four gas giants (shown here) are to scale. The distances between the planets are not to scale, however.

Saturn

Neptune

Uranus

Jupiter

A Day and a Year on Jupiter

Like every object in the solar system, Jupiter **orbits** the Sun. As it makes its journey around the Sun, it is traveling through space at just over 29,000 miles per hour (47,000 km/h).

Earth orbits the Sun once every 365 days, a time period we call a year. Jupiter is much further from the Sun, however, so it takes 4,333 days to make one full orbit. So a year on Jupiter lasts nearly 12 years! In that time, Jupiter makes a journey of 3,037,011,311 miles (4,887,595,931 km).

As the planets in the solar system orbit the Sun, each one also rotates, or spins, on its **axis**. Earth rotates once every 24 hours. Jupiter spins much faster than Earth, though, and takes just under 10 hours to make one full rotation.

Asteroids

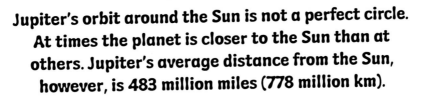

That's Out of This World!

Jupiter's orbit around the Sun is not a perfect circle. At times the planet is closer to the Sun than at others. Jupiter's average distance from the Sun, however, is 483 million miles (778 million km).

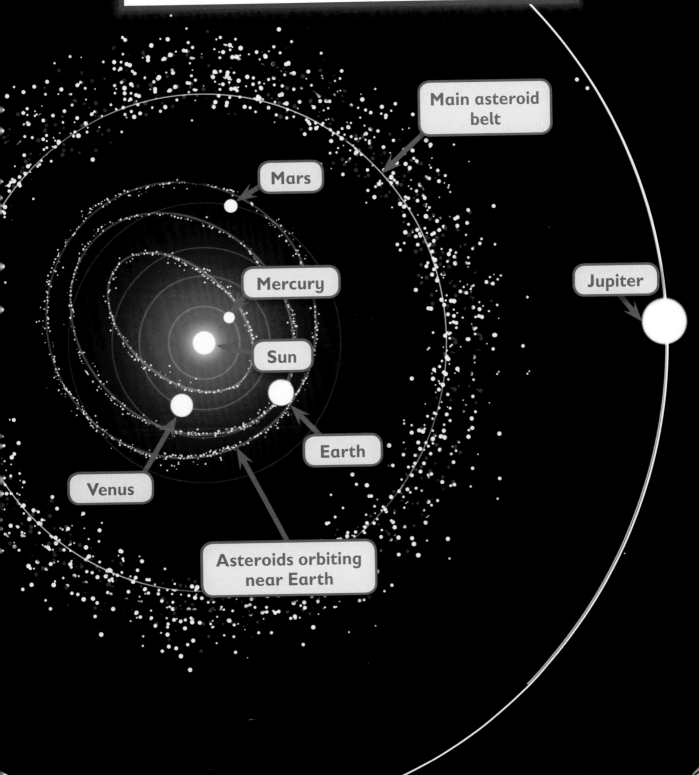

Main asteroid belt

Mars

Mercury

Jupiter

Sun

Earth

Venus

Asteroids orbiting near Earth

Inside a Gas Giant

Unlike the planet where we live, Jupiter has no outer solid surface. The planet is a massive ball of gases and liquids.

Jupiter is surrounded by a colorful layer of clouds. Below the clouds is a 600-mile-(1,000 km)-thick layer of hydrogen and helium gas. This gaseous layer is the planet's **atmosphere**.

Beneath the atmosphere is a layer made up of liquid hydrogen, which is about 12,500 miles (20,000 km) deep. Deeper into the planet, the pressure is so great that the liquid hydrogen actually becomes metallic, forming a 25,000-mile-(40,000 km)-deep layer of metallic liquid hydrogen. In the very center of the planet, scientists believe there may be a solid rocky core that is slightly larger than Earth.

That's Out of This World!

Hydrogen and helium are the same two gases that make up the Sun. So Jupiter has the same ingredients as a star. When it formed, however, Jupiter was too small to ignite in the way that our Sun did, so it lives out its life as a gas planet.

The layers of Jupiter

Layer of liquid hydrogen

Solid rock core

Layer of metallic liquid hydrogen

Clouds and atmosphere of gases

CLOUDS AND THE GREAT RED SPOT

When we look at Jupiter through a telescope, we see swirling white, orange, brown, and red clouds.

The layer of clouds surrounding Jupiter is about 30 miles (48 km) thick. The clouds are made mostly of the gas ammonia, with small quantities of **water vapor,** crystals of ice, and other **elements**.

Jupiter's best-known feature that can be seen through a telescope is a giant spinning storm called the Great Red Spot. This storm can be compared to a hurricane on Earth, but it is much larger than any hurricane on our planet. The vast, oval-shaped storm measures about 15,500 miles (25,000 km) by 7,500 miles (12,000 km). Inside the Great Red Spot swirling winds reach speeds of about 270 miles per hour (434 km/h).

Great Red Spot

The Great Red Spot is a massive, hurricane-like storm on Jupiter.

That's Out of This World!

No one knows when the Great Red Spot first appeared. It was observed by **astronomers** in the 1600s, however, when telescopes were first invented. So this massive hurricane has been raging for at least 400 years!

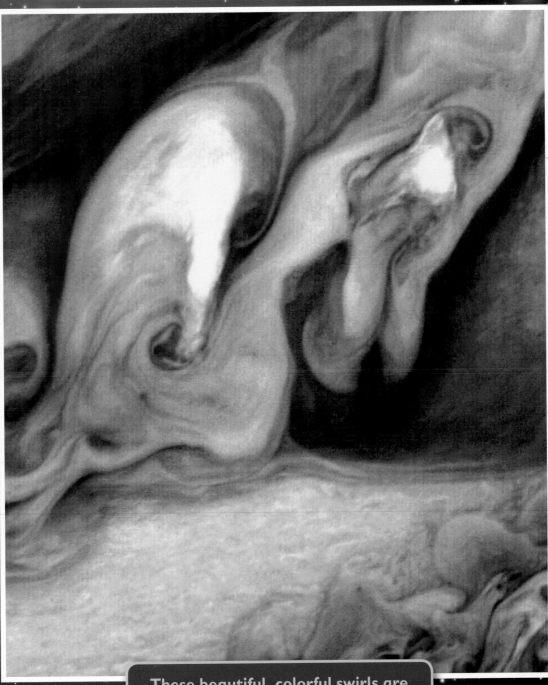

These beautiful, colorful swirls are clouds above Jupiter's atmosphere.

JUPITER'S MANY MOONS

A moon is a rocky object that orbits a planet. Mercury has no moons, Earth has just one, while Mars has two. Jupiter, however, has over 60 moons!

Jupiter's giant size means its gravity is very powerful. Over the billions of years of its life, it has pulled many rocky space objects into orbit around it.

The number of moons orbiting Jupiter is not definite, because when a new moon is discovered orbiting a planet, astronomers need to watch and track it for some time. Once they are sure the moon is permanently orbiting the planet, and is not just a rocky object temporarily passing the planet, the moon is named and becomes official. At the start of 2013, Jupiter had 50 confirmed, permanent moons. There are 16 other possible moons being watched and studied.

Jupiter's four largest moons are named Ganymede, Callisto, Europa, and Io. Ganymede is the largest moon in the solar system.

That's Out of This World!

Ganymede is larger than Mercury and the dwarf planet Pluto. If this giant moon were orbiting the Sun instead of orbiting Jupiter, it could be called a planet instead of a moon.

Io
Radius = 1,132 miles
(1,822 km)

Europa
Radius = 970 miles
(1,561 km)

Ganymede
Radius = 1,635 miles
(2,631 km)

Callisto
Radius = 1,498 miles
(2,411 km)

Jupiter's four largest moons are shown here with their sizes to scale. The moons' positions relative to each other are not to scale, however.

GANYMEDE, CALLISTO, AND EUROPA

Jupiter's giant moon Ganymede is covered by a thick outer shell of ice, which may be as thick as 497 miles (800 km).

Long grooves and ridges have formed in Ganymede's icy crust. Some of the ridges run for thousands of miles (km) and can be as high as mountains here on Earth.

Over time, the surfaces of most planets and moons change. This happens when superhot, liquid rock, called **lava**, spills onto the surface through cracks or **volcanoes**. The lava cools and hardens, forming rocks, changing the look of the land, and filling in **craters** formed when asteroids and other space objects crash into the surface of a planet or moon.

Jupiter's moon Callisto has not had this hot underground activity, however. With no lava to reshape the landscape, four billion years of impacts with other space bodies have left the moon's surface covered in craters.

That's Out of This World!

The surface of Jupiter's moon Europa is completely covered with a deep ocean. Because Europa is so far from the Sun, the water is frozen. Scientists believe, however, that deep below the thick ice, there could be liquid water.

EVER-CHANGING IO

Jupiter's moon Io has an ever-changing landscape because it is the most volcanically active body in the solar system.

As Io orbits Jupiter, the huge planet's gravity pulls at the little moon. This has a dramatic effect on the moon's surface.

If you've ever spent a day at the beach, you have seen how the ocean's water level rises and falls. This change in water levels, called the tide, is actually caused by the Moon's gravity pulling Earth's water toward it. A similar effect happens on Io, except that Io has no oceans, so Jupiter's gravity actually pulls at the rocky surface of Io, causing it to bulge up and down.

This pulling and stretching of Io's surface causes tremendous heat to build up, so there is always superhot, liquid rock below the moon's crust. As Io's surface bulges and stretches, lava from below the crust bursts onto the surface through cracks and volcanoes.

In November 1999, NASA's *Galileo* spacecraft captured this image of a volcanic eruption on Io (top left). At times, plumes of superhot material from volcanoes on Io are blasted nearly 200 miles (320 km) into the air!

Jupiter

Io

That's Out of This World!

Jupiter's gravitational pull can actually
cause the surface of Io to bulge outward by
as much as 300 feet (90 m).

WATCHING JUPITER

For around 4.5 billion years, the planets in our solar system have been orbiting the Sun, each taking its own path, or orbit, around our star.

Early astronomers with no telescopes or other equipment saw the planets as distant points of light. Ancient Greek astronomers noticed how the points of light moved in the night sky and named them *planetes*, which means "wanderers."

The ancient Romans also observed the planets Mercury, Venus, Mars, Jupiter, and Saturn. They named these bright objects after their gods. Jupiter was named after the king of the Roman gods.

When the telescope was invented in the early 1600s, astronomers were able to study the planets in more detail. One of these stargazers was the Italian astronomer Galileo Galilei. In 1610, Galileo discovered what he at first thought were four stars near Jupiter. He had, in fact, discovered Jupiter's four largest moons, Ganymede, Callisto, Io, and Europa.

That's Out of This World!

Jupiter's four largest moons are known today as the Galilean moons, or satellites, after their discoverer. A satellite is an object that orbits another body in space.

MISSIONS TO JUPITER

For hundreds of years, astronomers studied Jupiter through telescopes. Then, in March 1972, a spacecraft named *Pioneer 10* left Earth on a mission to study Jupiter.

As *Pioneer 10* flew past Jupiter, it transmitted hundreds of photos of the planet and its moons back to Earth. In December 1974, on its way to study Saturn, *Pioneer 11* also flew past Jupiter. Flying at 26,570 miles (42,760 km) above Jupiter's clouds, *Pioneer 11* captured the first ever pictures of Jupiter's **polar regions**.

In late summer 1977, *Voyager 1* and *Voyager 2* blasted off from Earth. Part of their missions was to study Jupiter as they passed the planet on their way to the outer reaches of the solar system. *Voyager 1* captured images of Ganymede, Callisto, Europa, and Io. This allowed astronomers to see the surfaces of these moons for the first time. *Voyager 1* also discovered that Io is home to many active volcanoes.

That's Out of This World!

Pioneer 10 and *Pioneer 11* are still in space today, heading toward the center of our **galaxy**. Each spacecraft carries a metallic plaque that shows where in the universe *Pioneer* was launched and what type of creatures built the spacecraft. These plaques are a message to any intelligent beings that may find the spacecraft.

One of the plaques attached to the *Pioneer* spacecraft, which carries a message from Earth to alien civilizations.

This artwork shows how *Pioneer 10* may have looked in space.

Discovering Jupiter's Rings

When the two *Voyager* spacecraft visited Jupiter in 1979, they captured images showing that Jupiter is surrounded by rings that are made up of dust and tiny pieces of rock.

There is one main ring encircling the planet that is about 4,300 miles (7,000 km) wide. Two of Jupiter's smaller moons, Adrastea and Metis, are orbiting Jupiter inside this ring. Scientists think that some of the rock and dust in the ring could be rubble created when other space bodies collided with the two moons.

On the inner edge of the main ring is the Halo. This ring is about 12,400 miles (20,000 km) thick. On the outer edge of the main ring is a ring of dust particles that are so small they would look no thicker than smoke. This outer ring is about 52,800 miles (85,000 km) wide.

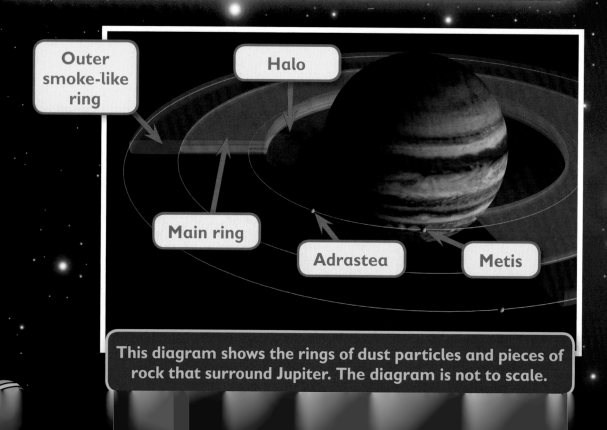

Outer smoke-like ring

Halo

Main ring

Adrastea

Metis

This diagram shows the rings of dust particles and pieces of rock that surround Jupiter. The diagram is not to scale.

That's Out of This World!

Astronomers suspected that Jupiter had rings, but *Voyager 1* confirmed they existed when it captured a single image showing the rings in March 1979. Scientists on Earth then reprogrammed *Voyager 2* so that it could take more pictures of the ring system when it reached the planet later that spring.

Artwork of a *Voyager* spacecraft

GALILEO GOES INTO SPACE

In October 1989, the NASA spacecraft *Galileo* was launched. Named for the astronomer who discovered Jupiter's largest moons, *Galileo* was carried into space aboard the space shuttle *Atlantis*.

In July 1995, when *Galileo* was still about 50 million miles (80 million km) from Jupiter, it released a probe that plunged into Jupiter's atmosphere. The probe examined Jupiter's clouds and studied the temperature, pressure, and chemical composition of Jupiter's atmosphere. The *Galileo* probe transmitted data back to the spacecraft for 58 minutes before it was crushed, melted, or vaporized by the extreme conditions in the gas giant's atmosphere.

In December 1995, *Galileo* entered Jupiter's orbit and began its study of the planet and its moons, which would last for nearly eight years. In that time, *Galileo* detected a belt of radiation above Jupiter's clouds and discovered that Jupiter has similar amounts of helium in its atmosphere as the Sun. It also found evidence that below Europa's icy surface there might be liquid water.

That's Out of This World!

As *Galileo* sped toward Jupiter in July 1994, a comet named Shoemaker-Levy 9 collided with the planet. Using equipment aboard *Galileo*, astronomers on Earth were able to observe what happens when a comet hits a gas giant planet. An impact between two objects in the solar system had never been witnessed before.

This artwork shows the *Galileo* probe descending into Jupiter's atmosphere.

Earth

Galileo

Space shuttle *Atlantis*

This artwork shows *Galileo* on its way to Jupiter after separating from the space shuttle *Atlantis*. The *Galileo* spacecraft was 15 feet (4.6 m) tall.

Juno, A Look Beneath the Clouds

As you read this book, NASA's *Juno* spacecraft is hurtling through space toward Jupiter. *Juno* launched in August 2011, and it will enter into orbit around Jupiter in July 2016.

During its planned one-year mission, *Juno* will orbit Jupiter 33 times. Even though Jupiter is hundreds of millions of miles (km) from the Sun, *Juno's* power will be provided by **solar panels** that will capture the Sun's energy.

Even though astronomers have been studying Jupiter for centuries, this faraway planet, hidden behind miles (km) of thick clouds, still holds many mysteries. Instruments aboard *Juno* will allow astronomers to see below Jupiter's thick clouds for the first time. *Juno* will study the gas giant's atmosphere and internal layers. It will also study how the gas giant formed. Studying Jupiter's formation will not only give scientists information about this planet, but will help answer many questions about how our entire solar system formed.

As the Sun rises on August 5, 2011, *Juno* is ready to launch aboard a rocket from Cape Canaveral Air Force Station in Florida.

This artwork shows *Juno* above the north pole of Jupiter. At times, *Juno* will be orbiting Jupiter just 3,100 miles (5,000 km) above the tops of the clouds.

That's Out of This World!

Juno is named after a Roman goddess. The goddess Juno was Jupiter's wife, and she had the power to see through clouds.

29

GLOSSARY

asteroids (AS-teh-roydz) Rocky objects orbiting the Sun and ranging in size from a few feet (m) to hundreds of miles (km) in diameter.

astronomers (uh-STRAH-nuh-merz) Scientists who specialize in the study of outer space.

atmosphere (AT-muh-sfeer) The layer of gases surrounding a planet, moon, or star.

axis (AK-sus) An imaginary line about which a body, such as a planet, rotates.

craters (KRAY-turz) A hole or dent in the surface of a planet or moon, usually caused by an impact with another space object.

elements (EH-luh-ments) Pure chemical substances that are found in nature. Hydrogen and helium are the most abundant elements in the universe, and iron is the most abundant element making up planet Earth.

equator (ih-KWAY-tur) An imaginary line drawn around a planet that is an equal distance from the north and south poles.

galaxy (GA-lik-see) A group of stars, dust, gas, and other objects held together in outer space by gravity.

gravity (GRA-vuh-tee) The force that causes objects to be attracted toward Earth's center or toward other physical bodies in space, such as stars or planets.

lava (LA-vuh) Rock that has been turned into a liquid or semiliquid by intense heat from within a planet, moon, or other planet-like object.

moons (MOONZ) A naturally occuring satellite of a planet

nebula (NEH-byuh-luh) A massive cloud of dust and gas in outer space. Many nebulae are formed by the collapse of stars, releasing matter that may, over millions or billions of years, clump together to form new stars.

orbits (OR-bits) To circle in a curved path around another object.

planet (PLA-net) An object in space that is of a certain size and that orbits, or circles, a star.

polar regions (POH-lur REE-junz)
The areas surrounding a planet's north
and south poles.

solar panels (SOH-ler PA-nulz)
A number of photovoltaic solar cells
joined together in flat panels that
absorb the Sun's energy so it can be
used as a source of power.

solar system (SOH-ler SIS-tem)
The Sun and everything that orbits
around it, including asteroids,
meteoroids, comets, and the planets
and their moons.

universe (YOO-nih-vers) All of the
matter and energy that exists as a
whole, including gravity and all the
planets, stars, galaxies, and contents of
intergalactic space.

volcanoes (vol-KAY-nohz) An opening
in the surface of a planet or moon,
often formed on a hill or a mountain,
from which lava can erupt.

water vapor (WAH-tur VAY-pur)
The state of water, caused by
evaporation, in which it ceases being
a liquid and becomes a gas.

WEBSITES

For web resources related to the subject of this book,
go to: www.windmillbooks.com/weblinks
and select this book's title.

READ MORE

Allyn, Daisy. *Jupiter: The Largest Planet*. Our Solar System. New York: Gareth Stevens Leveled Readers, 2010.

Richardson, Adele D. *Jupiter*. The Solar System. Mankato, MN: Capstone Press, 2008.

Sparrow, Giles. *Destination Jupiter*. Destination Solar System. New York: PowerKids Press, 2009.

INDEX